FRANCHISING IN RWANDA 2014

Legal and Business Considerations

KENDAL H. TYRE, JR., EXECUTIVE EDITOR
DIANA VILMENAY-HAMMOND, MANAGING EDITOR
COURTNEY L. LINDSAY, II, ASSISTANT EDITOR

LEXNOIR FOUNDATION

FIRST QUARTER 2014

LexNoir Foundation is the charitable, educational arm of LexNoir, an international network of lawyers connecting the African Diaspora.

This publication, *Franchising in Rwanda 2014: Legal and Business Considerations*, contains excerpts from *Franchising in Africa 2014: Legal and Business Considerations*. Both works are published by LexNoir Foundation and reflect the points of view of the authors and editors as of the date of publication and do not necessarily represent the opinions, interpretations, or positions of the law firms or organizations with which they are affiliated, nor the opinions, interpretations or positions of LexNoir Foundation or LexNoir.

Nothing contained in this book is to be considered as the rendering of legal advice, either generally or in connection with any specific issues or case. Readers are responsible for obtaining advice from their own legal counsel or other professional. This book, any forms and agreements or other information herein are intended for educational and informational purposes only.

www.lexnoir.org

Table of Contents

Franchising in Rwanda

Désiré Kamanzi
ENSafrica | Rwanda

Bibliography of International Franchise Resources

Kendal H. Tyre, Jr., Diana Vilmenay-Hammond, Pierce Haesung Han, Courtney L. Lindsay, II, and Keri McWilliams
Nixon Peabody LLP

Acknowledgment

This book could not have been written without the hard work and dedication of each of the contributing authors and editors. Thank you.

We would like to acknowledge and extend our heartfelt gratitude to Michael Collier and Maria Stallings of the Washington, D.C. office of Nixon Peabody LLP for their invaluable assistance in revising, proofing, and editing this publication.

About the Editors and Authors

Kendal H. Tyre, Jr. – Kendal is a partner in the Washington, D.C. office of Nixon Peabody LLP. He handles domestic and cross-border transactions, including mergers and acquisitions, joint ventures, strategic alliances, licensing, and franchise matters.

In his franchise and licensing practice, Kendal counsels domestic and international franchisors, franchisees, licensors, licensees and distributors regarding U.S. state and federal franchise laws as well as foreign franchise legislation in a variety of jurisdictions. Kendal drafts and provides advice with regard to franchise and license agreements, disclosure documents and area development agreements and has extensive experience drafting and negotiating a variety of other commercial agreements. His client base spans the United States and foreign countries, including South Africa, Kenya, and the United Kingdom.

Kendal is a frequent contributor to franchise publications and a frequent speaker at franchise programs held by the American Bar Association Forum on Franchising and the International Franchise Association.

Kendal is co-chair of the firm's Diversity Action Committee and its Africa Group. Kendal is also the executive director of LexNoir Foundation.

E-mail address: ktyre@nixonpeabody.com

Diana Vilmenay-Hammond – Diana is an attorney in the Washington, D.C. office of Nixon Peabody LLP. She is a member of the firm's Franchise & Distribution Team.

In her franchise practice, Diana works with domestic and international franchisors on transactional and litigation matters. Specifically, she counsels franchisor clients regarding state and federal franchise laws, disclosure and registration obligations.

Diana drafts and negotiates various commercial agreements, including international franchise and development agreements.

Diana has co-authored numerous articles on franchising and frequently co-hosted the Nixon Peabody franchise law webinar series. Topics have included:

- "Franchise Case Law Round-Up: Implications for Your Franchise," February 15, 2012;
- "Social Media Part II: Best Practices in Protecting Your Brand in the New Media," September 14, 2010; and
- "The Awuah Case: Bellwether or Outlier," May 11, 2010

Diana received her J.D. from Howard University School of Law and her B.A. from Georgetown University. She is a member of the American Bar Association (Forum on Franchising).

Email address: dvilmenay@nixonpeabody.com

Pierce Haesung Han – Pierce is an associate in Nixon Peabody's Global Business & Transactions Group. Pierce focuses his practice on three main areas, assisting clients with a variety of complex business transactions.

- Mergers & Acquisitions: Providing assistance to both public and private clients with various mergers and acquisitions, performing due diligence, drafting and negotiating transaction documents, and facilitating closing and post-closing mechanics.
- International Commercial Transactions: Drafting and negotiating a variety of commercial agreements, including international franchise and development agreements, license agreements, and purchase and sale agreements.
- Federal Securities Law Matters: Assisting public and private clients regarding federal securities laws and stock exchange rules relating to corporate governance and disclosure.

Pierce serves as the Secretary of the Asian Pacific Bar Association Educational Fund (an affiliate of the Asian Pacific American Bar Association of the Greater Washington, D.C. Area).

Pierce received his J.D. from Georgetown University Law Center and his B.A. from Case Western Reserve University. He is admitted to practice in the State of New York and the District of Columbia.

E-mail address: phan@nixonpeabody.com

Courtney L. Lindsay, II – Courtney is an associate in Nixon Peabody's Corporate and Finance practice. In his corporate practice, Courtney assists for-profit and non-profit entities with transactional matters and corporate governance. In various capacities, Courtney has been involved in multiple merger and acquisition transactions, including drafting and managing due diligence.

Previously, Courtney worked in the legal and business affairs department at a national cable network, where he handled matters related to the network's LLC agreement, including drafting board and member consent agreements.

Courtney received his J.D. from the University of Virginia School of Law and his B.A. from the University of Virginia. He is admitted to practice in the Commonwealth of Virginia and the District of Columbia.

E-mail address: clindsay@nixonpeabody.com

Keri McWilliams – Keri is an associate in the Franchise & Distribution team of Nixon Peabody LLP. Keri works with clients on a number of franchising issues, including obtaining and maintaining franchise registrations in various states, responding to state inquiries regarding trade practices, ongoing compliance with state and federal regulations, and updating franchise disclosure documents. She also handles franchise sales counseling and franchise system issues.

Keri is a member of the American Bar Association's Forum on Franchising, and the Federal and Minnesota State bar associations. She is also a member of Minnesota Women Lawyers and the Minnesota Association of Black Lawyers, and a volunteer in the Volunteer Lawyers Network.

Keri received her J.D. from the Georgetown University Law Center and her B.F.A. from Washington University. She is admitted to practice in the District of Columbia and Minnesota.

E-mail address: kmcwilliams@nixonpeabody.com

Désiré Kamanzi – Désiré is the head of ENSafrica | Rwanda and has 15 years experience practicing as an advocate in business law, including commercial law, contract law, banking and financial law, labor law, intellectual property law, mining law, telecommunication law, and ADR. His practice experience includes assisting leading local and international investors in establishing their businesses in Rwanda and acting for a number of major listed and unlisted clients in the mining, telecoms, transport and financial services sectors. Désiré serves as the Secretary General for the Rwandan Law Society and was previously the Chief Legal Counsel and Director for Trade & Investment Promotion of the country's Investment Promotion Authority. He has lectured at the law faculty of the National University of Rwanda and has been intricately involved in the drafting of certain identified key priority areas of the law in Rwanda. Désiré is recognized as a leading lawyer by the following reputable rating agency and its publication: Chambers and Partners - Global Guide to the World's Leading Lawyers 2013, 2012, 2011, 2010, 2009, 2008 – General Business Law (Rwanda)

E-mail address: dkamanzi@ensafrica.com

About the Book

Franchising in Rwanda 2014: Legal and Business Considerations contains excerpts from the larger work, *Franchising in Africa 2014: Legal and Business Considerations*. Both books serve as practical, succinct, easy-to-use reference tools for lawyers, business people and academics to use in navigating the myriad laws and business issues impacting franchise arrangements on the African continent.

This book provides an overview of the franchise industry in Rwanda and addresses the typical legal issues confronted when expanding a franchise system in Rwanda. The larger work, *Franchising in Africa 2014: Legal and Business Considerations*, covers those laws governing franchising in fifteen other African countries – Angola, Botswana, Burundi, Cape Verde, Democratic Republic of Congo, Egypt, Ethiopia, Ghana, Kenya, Mozambique, Nigeria, South Africa, Tunisia, Zambia and Zimbabwe.

In both books, an author, who is a legal expert in the designated jurisdiction, addresses the basic questions that a franchise lawyer would need to know to competently represent a client in expanding their franchise system to that country.

Each country chapter organizes a discussion of that country's laws under various headings and in a uniform format. Topics were sent to each country's author in the form of a questionnaire, and each author drafted responses to the questions presented. A general overview relating to the political and economic history of the country at the beginning of each chapter provides an initial context for the regulatory framework. [1]

---

[1] The source of information for these sections is the Central Intelligence Agency, https://www.cia.gov/library/publications/the-world-factbook/ (last visited November 3, 2013).

Apart from an overview of the legal framework for franchising, each book contains other articles and resources that should prove useful to those in the franchise industry.

The authors for each chapter are listed at the beginning of a chapter and their biographical information is listed in the previous section, *About the Editors and Authors*.

Readers should always consult with local counsel in the relevant jurisdiction instead of relying solely on the information contained in this book. The laws governing franchising are evolving and local counsel in Rwanda are best positioned to provide timely, relevant advice applying the current law to the particular facts of a case.

Franchising in Rwanda

Désiré Kamanzi

ENSafrica | Rwanda

Kigali, Rwanda

Rwanda

I.   Introduction

A.   Historical Background of Country

Rwanda held its first local elections in 1999 and its first post-genocide presidential and legislative elections in 2003. In 2009, Rwanda staged a joint military operation with the Congolese Army in the Democratic Republic of the Congo to rout out the Hutu extremist insurgency there and Kigali and Kinshasa restored diplomatic relations. Rwanda also jointed the Commonwealth of Nations in late 2009. Commonly known as the Commonwealth, it is an intergovernmental organization of 53 member states that were mostly territories of the former British Empire. In January 2013, Rwanda assumed a nonpermanent seat on the UN Security Council for the 2013-14 term.

B.   Economy of the Country

Rwanda is a rural country with about 90% of the population engaged in (mainly subsistence) agriculture and some mineral and agro-processing. Tourism, minerals, coffee and tea are Rwanda's main sources of foreign exchange. Minerals exports declined 40% in 2009-10 due to the global economic downturn. However, Rwanda has made substantial progress in stabilizing and rehabilitating its economy to pre-1994 levels. GDP has rebounded with an average annual growth of 7%-8% since 2003 and inflation has been reduced to single digits. Rwanda continues to receive substantial aid money and obtained IMF-World Bank Heavily Indebted Poor Country (HIPC) initiative debt relief in 2005-06. In recognition of Rwanda's successful management of its macro economy, in 2010, the IMF graduated Rwanda to a Policy Support Instrument (PSI). Rwanda also received a Millennium Challenge Threshold Program in 2008.

Africa's most densely populated country is trying to overcome the limitations of its small, landlocked economy by leveraging regional trade. Rwanda joined the East African Community and is aligning its budget, trade, and immigration policies with its regional partners. The government has embraced an expansionary fiscal policy to reduce poverty by improving education, infrastructure, and foreign and domestic investment and pursuing market-oriented reforms. The Rwandan government is seeking to become a regional leader in information and communication technologies.

In 2010, Rwanda neared completion of the first modern Special Economic Zone (SEZ) in Kigali. The SEZ seeks to attract investment in all sectors, but specifically in agribusiness, information and communications technologies, trade and logistics, mining, and construction. The global downturn hurt export demand and tourism, but economic growth has recovered, driven in large part by the services sector, but inflation has grown. On the back of this growth, the government is gradually ending its fiscal stimulus policy while protecting aid to the poor.

C.   Franchise Legal Overview

In Rwanda, there is no specific law that regulates franchise agreements and/or transactions. Nevertheless, the country has a strong willingness to unlock the opportunities in the franchising business area for Rwandans to exploit them.

Rwanda Development Board (RDB) and the Private Sector Federation (PSF) have set up a franchise association in the country, a move aimed at expanding businesses. The RDB and PSF seek to help entrepreneurs develop capacity to grow strong brands that can attract buyers.

II.   Regulatory Requirements

A.   Pre-Sale Disclosure

Please describe any pre-sale franchise disclosure or similar requirements that may apply to franchise transactions.

No pre-sale franchise disclosure or similar requirements apply to franchise transactions under the laws of Rwanda.

Rwanda

B.   Governmental Approvals, Registrations, Filing Requirements

Please describe any necessary government approvals, registrations, or filing requirements that may apply to franchise transactions.

Rwanda law is not prescriptive in regard to what formalities are required for a franchise transaction.

Notwithstanding the above, a Rwandan franchisor or franchisee will be subject to the regular registration procedures and filing requirements required for performing business activities in Rwanda, such as, inter alia, business registration with the Office of the Registrar General.

C.   Limits of Fees and Typical Term of Franchise Agreement

Please describe any limits upon the nature and extent of fees and the term of a typical franchise agreement.

In the absence of a specific legal framework governing franchise agreements, the parties are free to agree on the terms and conditions of a franchise agreement and to carry out their activities in circumstances and in a manner that does not contravene the existing laws of Rwanda.

III.   Currency

If all payments under a franchise agreement must be made in immediately available U.S. Dollars, please advise as to any restrictions, reporting requirements, or regulations concerning the exchange, repatriation, or remittance of U.S. Dollars.

There are no specific restrictions on payments made available in U.S. Dollars in Rwanda. However, these payments should not offend the Rwandan law on *Anti-Money Laundering and Combating the Financing of Terrorism.*

Rwanda

IV.   Taxes, Tariffs, and Duties

Please do not provide any in-depth comments on tax structuring. However, please provide your general comments on the typical amount of withholding tax that would apply and whether a "gross-up" provision contained in a franchise agreement would be enforceable in your country.

A.   Applicable Rate

A withholding tax of 15% is levied on the following payments made by resident individuals or resident entities including tax exempt entities:

1. dividends,

2. interests;

3. royalties;

4. service fees including management and technical service fees;

5. performance payments made to an artist, a musician or an athlete irrespective of whether paid directly or through an entity that is not resident in Rwanda;

6. lottery and other gambling proceeds.

The withholding agent is required to file a tax declaration and remit the tax withheld to the tax administration within 15 days after the tax is withheld.

According to Article 9 of the *Income Tax Act*,[2] a withholding tax of 5% of the value of goods imported for commercial use is payable at the customs on the CIF (Cost, Insurance and Freight) value before goods are released by customs.

---

[2]   *Law n°16/2005 of 18/08/2005 on Direct Taxes on Income* as amended to date.

4

Rwanda

A withholding tax of 3% on the sum invoices (excluding VAT) is retained by public institutions for supply of goods and services made to them based on public tenders.

B.   Gross-up Clauses

Gross-up provisions may be permissible as long as parties to a lawful agreement have mutual assent, full capacity to contract and the agreement was made in the absence of any duress or undue influence.

V.   Trademarks

Please advise us as to whether there are any special requirements for granting a valid trademark license, including the use of a registered user agreement or a short trademark license agreement and any required filing of such an agreement with the trademark authorities.

Intellectual property in Rwanda is regulated by *Law n° 31/2009 of 26/06/2009 on the Protection of Intellectual Property* ("IP Law").

Article 155 of the IP Law is the specific provision governing licensing agreements for trademarks. It stipulates that "[a]ny license contract relating to a registered mark or for which registration is requested shall provide that the licensor exercises effective control over the quality of the goods or services of the licensee, for which the mark is used. If the license contract does not provide for such quality control or the quality control is not actually exercised within the prescribed period and in the requisite manner, the license contract shall not be valid and may not be implemented."

The article also provides that to be enforceable against third parties, license agreements for registered marks must be recorded into the register of marks.

Rwanda

VI. Restrictions on Transfer

Please advise as to whether there are any restrictions (1) on a franchisor to restrict transfers by a master franchisee, any interest in a master franchisee, or the assets of the master franchisee or (2) the ability of a master franchisee to control and/or restrict transfers of a subfranchisee's rights under a master franchise agreement, interest in the subfranchisee, or the assets of the subfranchisee.

Rwandan Law does not specifically prescribe any specific restrictions on the franchisor's ability to restrict:

• transfers by a master franchisee;

• any interest in a master franchisee; or

• the assets of the master franchisee.

Nor do any restrictions exist relating to:

• the master franchisee's ability to control and/or restrict a subfranchisee:

• transfers of a subfranchisee's rights under a master franchise agreement;

• any interest in the subfranchisee; or

• the assets of the subfranchisee.

VII. Termination

Please advise us as to any laws relating to termination in your country, such as agency laws, required indemnity provisions, notice or "good cause" requirements, or other laws affecting termination of a franchise agreement. Please describe.

Rwanda

There are no laws regulating termination of franchise agreements in Rwanda.

Normally, in Rwanda, termination will arise upon the mutual agreement or by breach of performance of material contractual obligation by either of the parties.

Total breach of the contract gives right to damages based on the non-performed obligations.[3] Partial breach of the contract gives right to damages based on only part of remaining obligations to perform.[4]

VIII. Governing Law, Jurisdiction, and Dispute Resolution

A.   Choice of Law of Foreign Jurisdiction

Please confirm whether the choice of law of a foreign jurisdiction would likely to be upheld under the law of the country, except for certain matters such as trademarks, bankruptcy, and competition matters, which we assume would be governed by the law in your country.

Under Rwanda contract law,[5] the parties may freely declare their transactions to be subject to a particular jurisdiction of their choice, including foreign jurisdictions. The party's choice of law, however, must reflect a serious interest of the parties, have some connection with any of the elements of the agreement, or have some connection with the chosen foreign jurisdiction.

Under conflict of laws principles, a choice of foreign law will not be permissible when it would violate fundamental principles of Rwanda public policy and such foreign law is not capable of providing an alternative solution consistent with those principles.

---

[3]   Article 81 of the *Law n° 45/2011 of 25/11/2011 Governing Contracts.*

[4]   *Id.*

[5]   *Law n°45/2011 of 25/11/2011 governing Contracts.*

Rwanda

B.   International Arbitration Dispute Resolution

Please confirm that a court in your country would honor an election of international arbitration dispute resolution, and therefore refuse to hear any disputes arising under a franchise agreement.

Rwanda courts will generally give effect to the parties' right to freedom of contract, and to the legal system under which they choose to contract.

It is also noteworthy that Rwanda is a signatory of the *Convention on the Recognition and Enforcement of Foreign Arbitral Awards*[6] (the "New York Convention"). This means that Rwanda recognizes and enforces foreign arbitral awards.

The law in Rwanda regulating and governing arbitration is set out in the *Law n° 05/2010 of 10/01/2010* establishing the Kigali International Arbitration Center and determining its organization, functioning and competence. Upon a dispute arising, parties may choose their arbitrators or mediators in accordance with this law.

IX.   Non-Competition Provisions

If the franchise agreement prohibits the master franchisee from engaging in certain competitive activities during the term of the agreement, and for a 12-month period after the termination or expiration of the agreement, please comment on the enforceability of non-competition covenants in your country.

---

[6]   The *United Nations Commission on International Trade Law* (UNCITRAL) announced on November 3, 2008, that Rwanda has become the 143rd country to accede to the *Convention on the Recognition and Enforcement of Foreign Arbitral Awards*. The convention entered into force in Rwanda on January 29, 2009. Under the treaty, courts of the States Parties are required "to enforce arbitration agreements and to recognize and enforce arbitral awards made in other States."

Rwanda

Since there is no specific legal regime governing franchise agreements in Rwanda, the parties themselves may agree on non-competition provisions. However, such provisions shall not be against public policy of Rwanda law and should also not hinder others from engaging in competing in market forces.

X. Language Requirements

Does the law in your country require that a franchise agreement be translated into the local language in order to be enforceable between the parties?

Rwanda Legislation does not require that a franchise agreement be translated into local language in order to be enforceable between the parties. Please note however that Rwanda has three official languages: Kinyarwanda, French and English.

XI. Other Significant Matters

Please advise as to whether there are any significant matters not addressed above of which a franchisor should be aware in connection with its entering into a franchise agreement in your country.

There are no other significant matters to address.

Rwanda

Bibliography of International Franchise Resources

Kendal H. Tyre, Jr., Diana Vilmenay-Hammond, Pierce Haesung Han, Courtney L. Lindsay, II, and Keri McWilliams

Nixon Peabody LLP

Washington, D.C.

I. General International Resources

Mark Abell, Gary R. Duvall, and Andrea Oricchio Kirsh, *International Franchise Legislation* B1, ABA FORUM ON FRANCHISING (1996)

Kathleen C. Anderson and Anthony M. Stiegler, *Put Muscle in Your Marks: Enforcing Intellectual Property Rights* W14, ABA FORUM ON FRANCHISING (1995)

Richard M. Asbill and Jane W. LaFranchi, *International Franchise Sales Laws—A Survey* W7, ABA FORUM ON FRANCHISING (2005)

Jeffery A. Brimer, Alison C. McElroy, and John Pratt, *Going International: What Additional Restraints Will You Face?* W4, ABA FORUM ON FRANCHISING (2011)

Michael G. Brennan, Alexander Konigsberg, and Philip F. Zeidman, *Globetrotting: A Workshop on International Franchising* 10/W8, ABA FORUM ON FRANCHISING (1994)

Michael G. Brennan, Alexander Konigsberg, and Philip F. Zeidman, *Globetrotting: Strategies for Launching U.S. Franchisors Abroad* 2/P2, ABA FORUM ON FRANCHISING (1994)

Christopher P. Bussert and Jennifer Dolman, *Regaining Your Trademark After Abandonment or Misappropriation* W7, ABA FORUM ON FRANCHISING (2011)

Ronald T. Coleman and Linda K. Stevens, *Trade Secrets and Confidential Information: Rights and Remedies* W2, ABA FORUM ON FRANCHISING (2000)

Finola Cunningham, *Commerce Department Helps Franchisors Go Global*, in FRANCHISING WORLD 63 (Dec. 2005)

Michael R. Daigle and Alex S. Konigsberg, *Meeting Off-Shore Disclosure and Contract Requirements* F/W13, ABA FORUM ON FRANCHISING (1992)

Jennifer Dolman, Robert A. Lauer, and Lawrence M. Weinberg, *Structuring International Master Franchise Relationships for Success and Responding When Things Go Awry* W22, ABA FORUM ON FRANCHISING (2007)

Gary R. Duvall, Paul Jones, and Jane LaFranchi, *Planning for the International Enforcement of Franchise Agreements* W6, ABA FORUM ON FRANCHISING (1999)

William Edwards, *International Expansion: Do Opportunities Outweigh Challenges?* in FRANCHISING WORLD (February 2008)

George J. Eydt and Stuart Hershman, *Bringing a Foreign Franchise System to the United States* W9, ABA FORUM ON FRANCHISING (2009)

William A. Finkelstein and Louis T. Pirkey, *International Trademarks* W15, ABA FORUM ON FRANCHISING (1991)

William A. Finkelstein, *Protecting Trademarks Internationally: Current Strategies and Developments* B3, ABA FORUM ON FRANCHISING (1996)

Stephen Giles, Lou H. Jones, and Lawrence Weinberg, *Negotiating and Documenting Complex International Franchise Agreements* W21, ABA FORUM ON FRANCHISING (2006)

Steven M. Goldman, Stephen Giles, Marc Israel, and Stanley Wong, *Competition Round Up from Around the World* LB2, ABA FORUM ON FRANCHISING (2004)

David C. Gryce and E. Lynn Perry, *Trademarks and Copyrights in the International Arena* 6/W4, ABA FORUM ON FRANCHISING (1993)

Kenneth S. Kaplan, Andrew P. Loewinger, and Penelope J. Ward, *System Standards in International Franchising* W14, ABA FORUM ON FRANCHISING (2005)

Edward Levitt and Jorge Mondragon, *A Survey of International Legal Traps and How to Avoid Them—Beyond the Franchise Laws* W20, ABA FORUM ON FRANCHISING (2007)

Ned Levitt, Kendal H. Tyre, and Penny Ward, *The Impossible Dream: Controlling Your International Franchise System* W4, ABA FORUM ON FRANCHISING (2010)

Michael K. Lindsey and Andrew P. Loewinger, *International (Non-U.S.) Franchise Disclosure Requirements* W9, ABA FORUM ON FRANCHISING (2002)

Andrew P. Loewinger and John Pratt, *Recent Changes and Trends in International Franchise Laws* W4, ABA FORUM ON FRANCHISING (2008)

Andrew P. Loewinger and Thomas M. Pitegoff, *Avoiding the Long Arm of the Law in International Franchising: Issues and Approaches* W8, ABA FORUM ON FRANCHISING (1995)

Craig J. Madson and Katherine C. Spelman, *Similarity and Confusion in the Intellectual Property Arena* W11, ABA FORUM ON FRANCHISING (1997)

Christopher A. Nowak, John Pratt, and Carl E. Zwisler, *Franchising Internationally with Countries with Opaque Legal Systems* W20, ABA FORUM ON FRANCHISING (2006)

E. Lynn Perry and John L. Sullivan Jr., *Trademark Compliance and Enforcement Techniques* E/W12, ABA FORUM ON FRANCHISING (1992)

Marcel Portmann, *Franchising Sector Proves Global Reach*, in FRANCHISING WORLD (January 2007)

John Pratt and Luiz Henrique O. do Amaral, *Civil Law for Common Law Practitioners (or How to Draft an Agreement for Use Overseas)* W4, ABA FORUM ON FRANCHISING (2002)

Kirk W. Reilly, Robert F. Salkowski and Geoffrey B. Shaw, *Determining the Rules of Engagement in Litigation Here and Abroad* W5, ABA FORUM ON FRANCHISING (2008)

Catherine Riesterer and Frank Zaid, *Basics of International Franchising* L/B2, ABA FORUM ON FRANCHISING (1997)

W. Andrew Scott and Christopher N. Wormald, *Stranger in a Strange Land: Contrasting Franchising in International Expansion* W2, ABA FORUM ON FRANCHISING (2003)

Donald Smith and Erik Wulff, *International Franchising: The Unraveling of an International Franchise Relationship* 15/W13, ABA FORUM ON FRANCHISING (1993)

Frank Zaid, Pamela Mills, and Michael Santa Maria, *Essential Issues in International Franchising* LB/1, ABA FORUM ON FRANCHISING (2001)

II.   African Resources

Joyce G. Mazero and J. Perry Maisonneuve, *Franchising in the Middle East and North Africa* W2, ABA FORUM ON FRANCHISING (2009)

Kendal H. Tyre, Jr. and Diana Vilmenay-Hammond, *Franchise World: A Burgeoning Middle Class Spurs Franchise Investment in Africa*, MINORITY BUSINESS ENTREPRENEUR (November 2012)

Kendal H. Tyre, Jr., *IP Protection May Promote Additional Franchise Growth in Africa*, NIXON PEABODY LLP: FRANCHISING BUSINESS & LAW ALERT (September 2012)

Kendal H. Tyre, Jr., *Market Potential for Franchising in Africa*, NIXON PEABODY LLP: FRANCHISING BUSINESS & LAW ALERT (June 2011)

Kendal H. Tyre, Jr. and Courtney L. Lindsay, II, *Continued Growth of Franchising in Africa*, NIXON PEABODY LLP: FRANCHISE LAW ALERT (April 2013)

Kendal H. Tyre, Jr. and Courtney L. Lindsay, II, *Pan African Franchise Federation Holds Inaugural Meeting*, NIXON PEABODY LLP: AFRICA ALERT (June 2013)

Kendal H. Tyre, Jr. and Courtney L. Lindsay, II, *White House Encouraging Private Investment and Transparency in Sub-Saharan Africa*, NIXON PEABODY LLP: AFRICA ALERT (August 2012)

Kendal H. Tyre, Jr. and Diana Vilmenay-Hammond, *African Economic Growth Impacts Franchising on the Continent*, NIXON PEABODY LLP: FRANCHISE LAW ALERT (July 2012)

Kendal H. Tyre, Jr. and Diana Vilmenay-Hammond, *Franchising in Africa*, in FRANCHISING WORLD (August 2013)

John Sotos and Sam Hall, *African Franchising: Cross-Continent Momentum*, in FRANCHISING WORLD (June 2007)

A.   Angola

João Afonso Fialho, *Franchising in Angola*, in FRANCHISING IN AFRICA: LEGAL AND BUSINESS CONSIDERATIONS 91-105 (Kendal H. Tyre, Jr. & Diana Vilmenay-Hammond eds. 2012)

B.   Botswana

Bonzo Makgalemele, *Franchising in Botswana*, in FRANCHISING
IN AFRICA: LEGAL AND BUSINESS CONSIDERATIONS 107-117
(Kendal H. Tyre, Jr. & Diana Vilmenay-Hammond eds. 2012)

C.   Cape Verde

João Afonso Fialho, *Franchising in Cape Verde*, in
FRANCHISING IN AFRICA: LEGAL AND BUSINESS
CONSIDERATIONS 119-132 (Kendal H. Tyre, Jr. & Diana
Vilmenay-Hammond eds. 2012)

D.   Egypt

Girgis Abd El-Shahid, *Franchising in Eqypt*, in FRANCHISING IN
AFRICA: LEGAL AND BUSINESS CONSIDERATIONS 133-142
(Kendal H. Tyre, Jr. & Diana Vilmenay-Hammond eds. 2012)

A. Safaa El Din El Oteifi, *Egypt*, in INTERNATIONAL
FRANCHISING EGY/1 (Dennis Campbell gen. ed. 2011)

E.   Ethiopia

Yohannes Assefa and Biset Beyene Molla, *Franchising in
Ethiopia*, in FRANCHISING IN AFRICA: LEGAL AND BUSINESS
CONSIDERATIONS 143-157 (Kendal H. Tyre, Jr. & Diana
Vilmenay-Hammond eds. 2012)

Kendal H. Tyre, Jr., Yohannes Assefa and Getachew Mengistie
Alemu, *New Intellectual Property Regulation Requires Scramble
to Protect Marks in Ethiopia*, NIXON PEABODY LLP: AFRICA
ALERT (October 2013)

F.   Ghana

Divine K.D. Letsa and Hawa Tejansie Ajei, *Franchising in
Ghana*, in FRANCHISING IN AFRICA: LEGAL AND BUSINESS
CONSIDERATIONS 159-167 (Kendal H. Tyre, Jr. & Diana
Vilmenay-Hammond eds. 2012)

G.   Libya

Kendal H. Tyre, Jr. & Diana Vilmenay-Hammond, *First U.S. Franchise Opens in Libya*, NIXON PEABODY LLP: AFRICA ALERT (August 2012)

H.   Mozambique

Diogo Xavier da Cunha, *Franchising in Mozambique*, in FRANCHISING IN AFRICA: LEGAL AND BUSINESS CONSIDERATIONS 169-182 (Kendal H. Tyre, Jr. & Diana Vilmenay-Hammond eds. 2012)

I.   Nigeria

Theo Emuwa and Bimbola Fowler-Ekar, *Franchising in Nigeria*, in FRANCHISING IN AFRICA: LEGAL AND BUSINESS CONSIDERATIONS 183-198 (Kendal H. Tyre, Jr. & Diana Vilmenay-Hammond eds. 2012)

Kendal H. Tyre, Jr. and Theo Emuwa, *Nigerian Franchising: Making Your Way Through the Thicket*, NIXON PEABODY LLP: FRANCHISE LAW ALERT (June 2005)

J.   South Africa

Eugene Honey, *Franchising and the New Consumer Protection Bill*, BOWMAN GILFILLAN (March 2008)

Eugene Honey, *Franchising and the Consumer Protection Bill*, BOWMAN GILFILLAN (May 2008)

Eugene Honey, *Pitfalls and Difficulties with the CPA*, ADAMS & ADAMS (March 2013)

Eugene Honey, *Disclosure is Compulsory*, ADAMS & ADAMS (May 2013)

Eugene Honey and Wim Alberts, *Fundamental Consumer Rights: The Right to Equality*, BOWMAN GILFILLAN (March 2009)

Eugene Honey and Wim Alberts, *The Reach of the Consumer Protection Bill: The Final*, BOWMAN GILFILLAN (March 2009)

Eugene Honey, *South Africa*, in GETTING THE DEAL THROUGH: FRANCHISE (2013) 172-178 (Philip F. Zeidman ed. 2013)

Taswell Papier, *Franchising in South Africa*, in FRANCHISING IN AFRICA: LEGAL AND BUSINESS CONSIDERATIONS 199-224 (Kendal H. Tyre, Jr. & Diana Vilmenay-Hammond eds. 2012)

Kendal H. Tyre, Jr., *A New Legal Landscape for Franchising in South Africa*, NIXON PEABODY LLP: FRANCHISING BUSINESS & LAW ALERT (September 2009)

K.   Tunisia

Yessine Ferah, *Franchising in Tunisia*, in FRANCHISING IN AFRICA: LEGAL AND BUSINESS CONSIDERATIONS 225-245 (Kendal H. Tyre, Jr. & Diana Vilmenay-Hammond eds. 2012)

Kendal H. Tyre, Jr., Diana Vilmenay-Hammond, and Yessine Ferah, *New Franchise Legislation in Tunisia*, NIXON PEABODY LLP: FRANCHISE LAW ALERT (September 2010)

L.   Zambia

Mabvuto Sakala, *Franchising in Zambia*, in FRANCHISING IN AFRICA: LEGAL AND BUSINESS CONSIDERATIONS 247-255 (Kendal H. Tyre, Jr. & Diana Vilmenay-Hammond eds. 2012)

www.ingramcontent.com/pod-product-compliance
Lightning Source LLC
Chambersburg PA
CBHW060326220326
41598CB00027B/4430